The Vision of
Saint Paul the Apostle

By Paul

Copyright © 2021 Lamp of Trismegistus. All rights reserved. No part of this publication may be reproduced or transmitted in any form or by any means, electronic or mechanical, including photocopying, recording, or by any information storage and retrieval system, without permission in writing from Lamp of Trismegistus. Reviewers may quote brief passages.

ISBN: 978-1-63118-526-7

Christian Apocrypha Series

Other Books in this Series and Related Titles

The Book of Wisdom of Solomon by King Solomon (978-1-63118-502-1)

The Gospel of the Nativity of Mary by St. Matthew (978-1-63118-448-2)

The Hymn of Jesus by G. R. S. Mead (978-1-63118-409-3)

Psalms of Solomon by King Solomon (978-1-63118-439-0)

The First and Second Gospels of the Infancy of Jesus Christ (978-1-63118-415-4)

The Book of Parables by Enoch (978-1-63118-429-1)

The Testament of Abraham by Abraham (978-1-63118-441-3)

The Lives of Adam and Eve by Moses (978-1-63118-414-7)

Masonic Symbolism of King Solomon's Temple by A Mackey &c (978-1-63118-442-0)

The Secrets of Enoch by Enoch (978-1-63118-449-9)

Lost Chapters of the Book of Daniel and Related Writings (978-1-63118-417-8)

The Testament of Moses by Moses (978-1-63118-440-6)

The Book of the Watchers by Enoch (978-1-63118-416-1)

Buddhist Psalms by Shinran (978-1-63118-465-9)

Masonic Symbolism of Easter and the Christ in Masonry (978-1-63118-434-5)

The Odes of Solomon by King Solomon (978-1-63118-503-8)

Book of Dreams by Enoch (978-1-63118-437-6)

A Few Masonic Sermons by A. C. Ward &c (978-1-63118-435-2)

Catholicism, Yoga and Hinduism by Hartmann &c (978-1-63118-478-9)

The Hymns of Hermes by G. R. S. Mead (978-1-63118-405-5)

The Book of Astronomical Secrets by Enoch (978-1-63118-443-7)

Audio Versions are also Available on Audible, Amazon and Apple

INTRODUCTION

The Apocrypha are a loosely knit series of books, written by early vanguards of Christianity (covering the eras of both the old and new testaments), and which comprise somewhere between about a dozen to several hundred titles, depending on whom you ask and how that person defines "Apocrypha." A small selection of these can still be found included in the Catholic bible, while a majority of the books in question, were abandoned by church officials in the early centuries of Christianity. Many of these apocryphal books were originally considered canon by early followers of Christ, in the first four centuries following his birth. It wasn't until the meeting of the Council of Nicaea in 325, that Emperor Constantine and a group of roughly 300 church bishops, gathered together with the goal of defining, standardizing and unifying an otherwise splintering Christianity, that many of these writings ceased to be included in the newly established canon. Enjoy then, this book as an example, of just one of the many books of the Christian Apocrypha, and be sure to check out other titles in this series.

THE REVELATION
OR
VISION OF SAINT PAUL THE APOSTLE

Here Begins the Vision of Saint Paul the Apostle:

"But I will come to visions and revelations of the Lord: I know a man in Christ fourteen years ago (whether in the body, I know not; or out of the body, I know not, God knoweth) snatched up in this manner to the third heaven: and I know such a man, whether in the body or out of the body I know not, God knoweth; how that he was snatched up into Paradise and heard secret words which it is not lawful for men to speak; on behalf of such a one will I glory; but on mine own behalf I will not glory, save in my infirmities."
-2 Corinthians 12:1-5

1. At what time was this revelation made? In the consulship of Theodosius Augustus the Younger and Cynegius, a certain nobleman then living in Tharsus, in the house which was that of Saint Paul, an angel appearing in the night revealed to him, saying that he should open the foundations of the house and should publish what he found, but he thought that these things were dreams;

2. But the angel coming for the third time beat him and forced him to open the foundation. And digging he found a marble box, inscribed on the sides; there was the revelation of Saint Paul, and his shoes in which he walked teaching the word of God. But he feared to open that box and brought it to the judge; when he had received it, the judge, because it was sealed with lead, sent it to the Emperor Theodosius, fearing lest it might be something else; which when he had received the emperor opened it, and found the revelation of Saint Paul; a

copy of it he sent to Jerusalem, and retained the original himself.

3. While I was in the body in which I was snatched up to the third heaven, the word of the Lord came to me saying: speak to the people: until when will ye transgress, and heap sin upon sin, and tempt the Lord who made you? Ye are the sons of God, doing the works of the devil in the faith of Christ, on account of the impediments of the world. Remember therefore and know that while every creature serves God, the human race alone sins. But it reigns over every creature and sins more than all nature.

4. For indeed the sun, the great light, often addressed the Lord saying: Lord God Almighty, I look out upon the impieties and injustices of men; permit me and I shall do unto them what are my powers, that they may know that thou art God alone. And there came a voice saying to him: I know all these things, for mine eye sees and ear hears, but my patience bears them until they shall be converted and repent. But if they do not return to me I will judge them all.

5. For sometimes the moon and stars addressed the Lord saying: Lord God Almighty, to us thou hast given the power of the night; till when shall we look down upon the impieties and fornications and homicides done by the sons of men? Permit us to do unto them according to our powers, that they may know that thou art God alone. And there came a voice unto them saying: I know all these things, and mine eye looks forth and ear hears, but my patience bears with them until they shall

be converted and repent. But if they do not return unto me I will judge them.

6. And frequently also the sea exclaimed saying: Lord God Almighty, men have defiled thy holy name in me; permit me to arise and cover every wood and orchard and the whole world, until I blot out all the sons of men from before thy face, that they may know that thou art God alone. And the voice came again and said: I know all things; mine eye seeth everything, and mine ear heareth, but my patience bears with them until they be converted and repent. But if they do not return, I will judge them. Sometimes the waters also spoke against the sins of men saying: Lord God Almighty, all the sons of men have defiled thy holy name. And there came a voice saying: I know all things before they come to pass, for mine eye seeth and mine ear heareth all things, but my patience bears with them until they be converted. But if not I will judge them. Frequently also the earth too exclaimed to the Lord against the sons of men saying: Lord God Almighty, I above every other creature of thine am harmed, supporting the fornications, adulteries, homicides, thefts, perjuries and magic and ill-doings of men and all the evil they do, so that the father rises up against the son, and the son upon the father, the alien against the alien, so that each one defiles his neighbour's wife. The father ascends upon the bed of his own son, and the son likewise ascends the couch of his own father; and in all these evils, they who offer the sacrifice to thy name have defiled thy holy place. Therefore I am injured above every creature, desiring not to shew my power to myself, and my fruits to the sons of men. Permit me and I will destroy the virtue of my fruits. And there came a voice and said: I know

all things, and there is none who can hide himself from his sin. Moreover I know their impieties, but my holiness suffers them until they be converted and repent. But if they do not return unto me I will judge them.

7. Behold, ye sons of men, the creature is subject to God, but the human race alone sins. For this cause, therefore, ye sons of men, bless the Lord God unceasingly, every hour and every day: but more especially when the sun has set: for at that hour all the angels proceed to the Lord to worship him and to present the works of men, which every man has wrought from the morning till the evening, whether good or evil. And there is a certain angel who proceeds rejoicing concerning the man in whom he dwells. When therefore the sun has set in the first hour of night, in the same hour the angel of every people and every man and woman, who protect and preserve them, because man is the image of God: similarly also in the matin hour which is the twelfth of the night, all the angels of men and women, go up to God to worship God, and present every work which each man has wrought, whether good or evil. Moreover every day and night the angels show to God an account of all the acts of the human race. To you, therefore, I say, ye sons of men, bless the Lord God without fail all the days of your life.

8. Therefore at the appointed hour all the angels whatever, rejoicing at once together, proceed before God that they may meet to worship at the hour determined. And behold suddenly it became the hour of meeting, and the angels came to worship in the presence of God, and the spirit proceeded to meet them:

and there came a voice and said: Whence come ye, our angels, bearing the burdens of tidings?

9. They answered and said: We come from those who have renounced this world for the sake of thy holy name, wandering as pilgrims, and in caves of the rocks, and weeping every hour in which they inhabited the earth, and hungering and thirsting because of thy name, with their loins girded, having in theist hands the incense of their hearts, and praying and blessing every hour, and restraining and overcoming themselves, weeping and wailing above the rest that inhabit the earth. And we indeed, their angels, mourn along with them: whither therefore it shall please thee, command us to go and minister, lest others also do it, but the destitute above the rest who are on earth. And there came the voice of God to them saying: Know ye that now henceforward my grace is appointed unto you, and my help, who is my well-beloved Son, shall be present with them, guiding them every hour; ministering also to them, never deserting them, since their place is his habitation.

10. When therefore these angels had retired, behold other angels came to adore in the presence of honour, in the assembly, who wept; and the spirit of God proceeded to meet them, and there came the voice of God and said: Whence come ye, our angels, bearing the burdens of the ministry of the tidings of the world? They answered and said in the presence of God: We have arrived from those who called upon thy name, and the impediments of the world made them wretched, devising many occasions every hour, not even making one pure prayer, nor out of their whole heart, in all the time of their life; what need,

therefore, is there to be present with men who are sinners? And there came the voice of God to them: It is necessary that ye should minister to them, until they be converted and repent: but if they do not return to me I will judge them. Know therefore, sons of men, that whatever things are wrought by you, these angels relate to God, whether good or evil.

11. And the angel answered and said unto me: Follow me, and I will show you the place of the just where they are led when they are deceased, and after these things taking thee into the abyss, I will show thee the souls of sinners and what sort of place they are led into when they have deceased. And I proceeded back after the angel, and he led me into heaven, and I looked back upon the firmament, and I saw in the same place power, and there was there oblivion which deceives and draws down to itself the hearts of men, and the spirit of detraction, and the spirit of fornication, and the spirit of madness, and the spirit of insolence, and there were there the princes of vices: these I saw under the firmament of heaven: and again I looked back, and I saw angels without mercy, having no pity, whose countenance was full of madness, and their teeth sticking out beyond the mouth: their eyes shone like the morning star of the east, and from the hairs of their head sparks of fire went out, or from their mouth. And I asked the angel saying: Sir, who are those? And the angel answered and said unto me: These are those who are destined to the souls of the impious in the hour of need, who did not believe that they had the Lord for their helper, nor hoped in him.

12. And I looked on high and I saw other angels whose countenance shone as the sun, their loins girded with golden girdles, having palms in their hands, and the sign of God, clothed with garments in which was written the name of the Son of God, filled moreover with all meekness and pity; and I asked the angels saying: Who are these, Lord, in so great beauty and pity? And the angel answered and said unto me: These are the angels of justice who are sent to lead up the souls of the just, in the hour of need, who believed that they had the Lord for their helper. And I said to him: Do the just and sinners necessarily meet witnesses when they have died? And the angel answered and said to me: There is one way by which all pass over to God, but the just having their helper with them are not confounded when they go to appear in the sight of God.

13. And I said to the angel: I wished to see the souls of the just and of sinners going out of the world. And the angel answered and said unto me: Look down upon the earth. And I looked down from heaven upon the earth, and saw the whole world, and it was nothing in my sight and I saw the sons of men as though they were naught, and a-wanting, and I wondered and said to the angel: Is this the greatness of men? And the angel answered and said unto me: It is, and these are they who do evil from morning till evening. And I looked and saw a great cloud of fire spread over the whole world, and I said to the angel: What is this, my Lord? and he said to me: This is injustice stirred up by the princes of sinners.

14. I indeed when I had heard this sighed and wept, and said to the angel: I wished to see the souls of the just and of

sinners, and to see in what manner they go out of the body. And the angel answered and said unto me: Look again upon the earth. And I looked and saw all the world, and men were as naught and a-wanting: and I looked carefully and saw a certain man about to die, and the angel said to me: This one whom thou seest is a just man. And I looked again and saw all his works, whatever he had done for the sake of God's name, and all his desires, both what he remembered, and what he did not remember; they all stood in his sight in the hour of need; and I saw the just man advance and find refreshment and confidence, and before he went out of the world the holy and the impious angels both attended: and I saw them all, but the impious found no place of habitation in him, but the holy took possession of his soul, guiding it till it went out of the body: and they roused the soul saying: Soul, know thy body whence thou goest out, for it is necessary that thou shouldst return to the same body on the day of the resurrection, that thou mayest receive the things promised to all the just. Receiving therefore the soul from the body, they immediately kissed it as familiarly known to them, saying to it: Do manfully, for thou hast done the will of God while placed in the earth. And there came to meet him the angel who watched him every day, and said to him: Do manfully, soul; for I rejoice in thee, because thou hast done the will of God on earth: for I related to God all thy works, such as they were. Similarly also the spirit proceeded to meet him and said: Soul, fear not, nor be disturbed, until thou comest into a place which thou hast never known, but I will be a helper unto thee: for I found in thee a place of refreshment in the time when I dwelt in thee, while I was on earth. And his spirit strengthened him, and his angel received him, and led him into heaven: and an angel said: Whither runnest thou, O soul, and dost thou dare to enter into heaven? Wait and let us see if there is anything of ours in thee: and behold we find nothing in thee. I see also thy divine helper and angel, and the spirit is rejoicing along with thee, because thou hast done the will of God on earth. And they led him along till he should worship in the sight of God. And when they had ceased, immediately Michael and all the army of angels, with one voice, adored the footstool of his feet, and his doom, saying at the same time to the soul: This is your God of all things, who made you in his own image and likeness. Moreover the angel returns and points him out saying: God, remember his labours: for this is the soul, whose works I related to thee, doing according to thy judgment. And the spirit said likewise: I am the spirit of vivification inspiring him: for I had refreshment in him, in the time when I dwelt in him, doing according to thy judgment. And there came the voice of God and said: In as much as this man did not vex me, neither will I vex him; for according as he had pity, I also will have pity. Let him therefore be handed over to Michael, the angel of the Covenant, and let him lead him into the Paradise of joy, that he himself may become co-heir with all the saints. And after these things I heard the voices of a thousand thousand angels, and archangels, and cherubim, and twenty-four elders saying hymns, and glorifying the Lord and crying: thou art just, O Lord, and just are thy judgments, and there is no acceptance of persons with thee, but thou rewardest unto every man according to thy judgment. And the angel answered and said unto me: Hast thou believed and known, that whatever each man of you has done, he sees in the hour of need? And I said: Yes, sir.

15. And he saith to me: Look again down on the earth, and watch the soul of an impious man going out of the body, which vexed the Lord day and night, saying: I know nothing else in this world, I eat and drink, and enjoy what is in the world; for who is there who has descended into hell, and ascending has declared to us that there is judgment there! And again I looked carefully, and saw all the scorn of the sinner, and all that he did, and they stood together before him in the hour of need: and it was done to him in that hour, in which he was threatened about his body at the judgment, and I said: It were better for him if he hall not been born. And after these things, there came at the same time, the holy angels, and the malign, and the soul of the sinner and the holy angels did not find a place in it. Moreover the malign angels cursed it; and when they had drawn it out of the body, the angels admonished it a third time, saying: O wretched soul, look upon thy flesh, whence thou camest out: for it is necessary that thou shouldst return to thy flesh in the day of resurrection, that thou mayest receive the due for thy sins and thy impieties.

16. And when they had led it forth, the customary angel preceded it, and said to it: O wretched soul, I am the angel belonging to thee, relating daily to the Lord thy malign works, whatever thou didst by night or day: and if it were in my power, not for one day would I minister to thee, but none of these things was I able to do: the judge is pitiful and just, and he himself commanded us that we should not cease to minister to the soul, till you should repent, but thou hast lost the time of repentance. I indeed was strange to thee and thou to me. Let

us go on then to the just judge: I will not dismiss thee, before I know from to-day why I was strange to thee. And the spirit confounded him, and the angel troubled him. When, therefore, they had arrived at the power, when he started to enter heaven, a labour was imposed upon him, above all other labour: error and oblivion and murmuring met him, and the spirit of fornication, and the rest of the powers, and said to him: Whither goest thou, wretched soul, and darest thou to rush into heaven? hold, that we may see if we have our qualities in thee, since we do not see that thou hast a holy helper. And after that I heard voices in the height of heaven saying: Present that wretched soul to God, that it may know that it is God that it despised. When, therefore, it had entered heaven, all the angels saw it, a thousand thousand exclaimed with one voice, all saying: Woe to thee, wretched soul, for the sake of thy works which thou didst on earth; what answer art thou about to give to God when thou shalt have approached to adore him? The angel who was with it answered and said: Weep with me, my beloved, for I have not found rest in this soul. And the angels answered him and said: Let such a soul be taken away from the midst of ours, for from the time he entered, the stink of him crosses to us angels. And after these things it was presented, that it might worship in the sight of God, and an angel of God showed him God who made him after his own image and likeness. Moreover his angel ran before him saying: Lord God Almighty, I am the angel of this soul, whose works I presented to thee day and night, not doing according to thy judgment. And the spirit likewise said: I am the spirit who dwelt in it from the time it was made, in itself moreover I know it, and it has not followed my will: judge it, Lord, according to thy judgment.

And there came the voice of God to it and said: Where is thy fruit which thou has made worthy of the goods which thou hast received? Have I put a distance of one day between thee and the just man? Did I not make the sun to arise upon thee as upon the just? But the soul was silent, having nothing to answer: and again there came a voice saying: Just is the judgment of God, and there is no acceptance of persons with God, for whoever shall have done mercy, on them shall he have mercy, and whoever shall not have pitied neither shall God pity him. Let him therefore be handed over to the angel Tartaruch, who is set over the punishments, and let him place him in outer darkness, where there is weeping and gnashing of teeth, and let him be there till the great day of judgment. And after these things I heard the voice of angels and archangels saying: Thou art just, Lord, and thy judgment is just.

17. And again I saw, and behold a soul which was led forward by two angels, weeping and saying: Have pity on me, just God, God the judge, for to-day is seven days since I went out of my body, and I was handed over to these two angels, and they led me through to those places, which I had never seen. And God, the just judge, saith to him: What hast thou done? for thou never didst mercy, wherefore thou wast handed over to such angels as have no mercy, and because thou didst not do uprightly, so neither did they act piously with thee in the hour of thy need. Confess therefore thy sins which thou didst commit when placed in the world. And he answered and said: Lord, I did not sin. And the Lord, the just Lord, was angered in fury when it said: I did not sin, because it lied; and God said: Dost thou think thou art still in the world? if any one of you,

sinning there, conceal and hide his sin from his neighbour, here indeed nothing whatever shall be hid: for when the souls come to adore in sight of the throne, both the good works and the sins of each one are made manifest. And hearing these things the soul was silent, having no answer. And I heard the Lord God, the just judge, again saying: Come, angel of this soul, and stand in the midst. And the angel of the sinful soul came, having in his hands a manuscript, and said: These, Lord, in my hands, are all the sins of this soul from his youth till to-day, from the tenth year of his birth: and if thou command, Lord, I will also relate his acts from the beginning of his fifteenth year. And the Lord God, the just judge, said: I say unto thee, angel, I do not expect of thee an account of him since he began to be fifteen years old, but state his sins for five years before he died and before he came hither. And again God, the just judge, said: For by myself I swear, and by my holy angels, and by my virtue, that if he had repented five years before he died, on account of one year's life, oblivion would now be thrown over all the evils which he sinned before, and he would have indulgence and remission of sins: now indeed he shall perish. And the angel of the sinful soul answered and said: Lord, command that angel to exhibit those souls.

18. And in that same hour the souls were exhibited in the midst, and the soul of the sinner knew them; and the Lord said to the soul of the sinner: I say unto thee, soul, confess thy work which thou wroughtest in these souls, whom thou seest, when they were in the world. And he answered and said: Lord, it is not yet a full year since I slew this one and poured his blood upon the ground, and with another (a woman) I committed

fornication: not this alone, but I also greatly harmed her in taking away her goods. And the Lord God, the just judge, said: Either thou didst not know that he who does violence to another, if he dies first who sustains the violence, is kept in this place until the doer of hurt dies, and then both stand in the presence of the judge, and now each receives according to his deed. And I heard a voice of one saying: Let that soul be delivered into the hands of Tartarus, and led down into hell: he shall lead him into the lower prison and he shall be put in torments, and left there till the great day of judgment. And again I heard a thousand thousand angels saying hymns to the Lord, and crying: Thou art just, O Lord, and just are thy judgments.

19. The angel answered and said unto me: Hast thou perceived all these things? and I said, Yes, sir. And he said to me: Follow me again, and I will take thee, and show thee the places of the just. And I followed the angel, and he raised me to the third heaven, and placed me at the entry of the door: and looking carefully I saw, and the door was of gold, and two columns of gold, full above of golden letters, and the angel tuned again to me and said: Blessed weft thou, if thou hadst entered into these doors, for it is not allowed to any to enter except only to those who have goodness and innocence of body in all things. And I asked the angel about everything and said: Sir, tell me on what account these letters are put upon those tables? The angel answered and said unto me: These are the names of the just, serving God with their whole heart, who dwell on the earth. And again I said: Sir, therefore their names and countenance and the likeness of these who serve God are

in heaven, and are known to the angels: for they know who are the servants of God with all their heart, before they go out of the world.

20. And when I had entered the interior of the gate of Paradise, there came out to meet me an old man whose countenance shone as the sun; and when he had embraced me he said: Hail, Paul, beloved of God. And he kissed me with a cheerful countenance. He wept, and I said to him: Brother, why dost thou weep? And again sighing and lamenting he said: We are hurt by men, and they vex us greatly; for many are the good things which the Lord has prepared, and great is his promise, but many do not perceive them. And I asked the angel, and said: Sir, who is this? And he said to me: This is Enoch, the scribe of righteousness. And I entered into the interior of that place, and immediately I saw the sun, and coming it saluted me laughing and rejoicing. And when it had seen (me), it turned away and wept, and said to me: Paul, would that thou shouldst receive thy labours which thou hast done in the human race. For me, indeed, I have seen the great and many good things, which God has prepared for the just, and the promises of God are great, but many do not perceive them; but even by many labours scarcely one or two enters into these places.

21. And the angel answered and said to me, Whatever I now show thee here, and whatever thou shalt hear, tell it not to anyone in the earth. And he led me and shewed me: and there I heard words which it is not lawful for a man to speak. And again he said, For now follow me, and I will shew thee what thou oughtest to narrate in public and relate.

And he took me down from the third heaven, and led me into the second heaven, and again he led me on to the firmament and from the firmament he led me over the doors of heaven: the beginning of its foundation was on the river which waters all the earth. And I asked the angel and said, Lord, what is this river of water? and he said to me, This is Oceanus! And suddenly I went out of heaven, and I understood that it is the light of heaven which lightens all the earth. For the land there is seven times brighter than silver. And I said, Lord, what is this place? And he said to me, This is the land of promise. Hast thou never heard what is written: Blessed are the meek: for they shall inherit the earth? The souls therefore of the just, when they have gone out of the body, are meanwhile dismissed to this place. And I said to the angel, Then this land will be manifested before the time? The angel answered and said to me, When Christ, whom thou preachest, shall come to reign, then, by the sentence of God, the first earth will be dissolved and this land of promise will then be revealed, and it will be like dew or cloud, and then the Lord Jesus Christ, the King Eternal, will be manifested and will come with all his saints to dwell in it, and he will reign over them a thousand years, and they will eat of the good things which I shall now show unto thee.

22. And I looked around upon that land and I saw a river flowing of milk and honey, and there were trees planted by the bank of that river, full of fruit: moreover each single tree bore twelve fruits in the year, having various and diverse fruits: and I saw the created things which are in that place and all the work of God, and I saw there palms of twenty cubits, but others of

ten cubits: and that land was seven times brighter than silver. And there were trees full of fruits from the roots to the highest branches, of ten thousand fruits of palms upon ten thousand fruits. The grape-vines moreover had ten thousand plants. Moreover in the single vines there were ten thousand thousand bunches and in each of these a thousand single grapes: moreover these single trees bore a thousand fruits. And I said to the angel, Why does each tree bear a thousand fruits? The angel answered and said unto me, Because the Lord God gives an abounding flood of gifts to the worthy, because they also of their own will afflicted themselves when they were placed in the world doing all things on account of his holy name. And again I said to the angel, Sir, are these the only promises which the Most Holy God makes? And he answered and said to me: No! there are seven times greater than these. But I say unto thee that when the just go out of the body they shall see the promises and the good things which God has prepared for them. Till then, they shall sigh, and lament saying: Have we emitted any word from our mouth to vex our neighbour even on one day? I asked and said again: Are these alone the promises of God? And the angel answered and said unto me: These whom you now see are the souls of the married and those who kept the chastity of their nuptials, containing themselves. But to the virgins and those who hunger and thirst after righteousness and those who afflicted themselves for the sake of the name of God, God will give seven times greater than these, which I shall now show thee.

And then he took me up from that place where I saw these things and behold, a river, and its waters were greatly whiter than milk, and I said to the angel, What is this? And he said to me: This is the Acherousian Lake where is the City of Christ, but not every man is permitted to enter that city; for this is the journey which leads to God, and if anyone is a fornicator and impious, and is converted and shall repent and do fruits worthy of repentance, at first indeed when he shall have gone out of the body, he is led and adores God, and thence by command of the Lord he is delivered to the angel Michael and he baptizes him in the Acherousian Lake-thus he leads them into the City of Christ alongside of those who have never sinned. But I wondered and blessed the Lord God for all the things which I saw.

23. And the angel answered and said unto me: Follow me and I will lead thee into the City of Christ. And he was standing on the Acherousian Lake and he put me into a golden ship and angels as it were three thousand were saying hymns before me till I arrived at the City of Christ. Moreover those who inhabited the City of Christ greatly rejoiced over me as I went to them, and I entered and saw the City of Christ, and it was all of gold, and twelve walls encircled it, and twelve interior towers, and each wall had between them single stadia in the circuit: And I said to the angel, Sir, how much is a stadium? The angel answered and said to me: As much as there is between the Lord God and the men who are on the earth, for the City of Christ is alone great. And there were twelve gates in the circuit of the city, of great beauty, and four rivers which encircled it. There was, moreover, a river of honey and a river of milk, and a river of wine and a river of oil. And I said to the angel: What are these rivers surrounding that city? And he saith

to me: These are the four rivers which flow sufficiently for those who are in this land of promise, of which the names are: the river of honey is called Fison, and the river of milk Euphrates, and the river of oil Gion, and the river of wine Tigris, such therefore they are for those who when placed in the world did not use the power of these things, but they hungered for these things and afflicted themselves for the sake of the Lord God: so that when these enter into this city, the Lord will assign them these things on high above all measure.

24. I indeed entering the gates saw trees great and very high before the doors of the city, having no fruit but leaves only, and I saw a few men scattered in the midst of the trees, and they lamented greatly when they saw anyone enter the city. And those trees were sorry for them and humbled themselves and bowed down and again erected themselves. And I saw and wept with them and I asked the angel and said: Sir, who are these who are not admitted to enter into the City of Christ? And he said to me: These are they who zealously abstained day and night in fasts, but they had a proud heart above other men, glorifying and praising themselves and doing nothing for their neighbours. For they gave some friendly greeting, but to others they did not even say hail! and indeed they shewed hospitality to those only whom they wished, and if they did anything whatever for their neighbour they were immoderately puffed up. And I said: What then, Sir? Did their pride prevent them from entering into the City of Christ? And the angel answered and said unto me: Pride is the root of all evils. Are they better than the Son of God who came to the Jews with much humility? And I asked him and said: Why is it that the trees

humble themselves and erect themselves again? And the angel answered and said to me: The whole time which these men passed on earth zealously serving God, on account of the confusion and reproaches of men at the time, they blushed and humiliated themselves, but they were not saddened. nor did they repent that they should recede from their pride which was in them. This is why the trees humble themselves, and again are raised up. And I asked and said: For what cause were they admitted to the doors of the city? The angel answered and said unto me: Because of the great goodness of God, and because there is the entry of his holy men entering into this city: for this cause they are left in this place, but when Christ the King Eternal enters with his saints, as he enters just men may pray for these, and then they may enter into the city along with them: but yet none of them is able to have assurance such as they have who humbled themselves, serving the Lord God all their lives.

25. But I went on while the angel instructed me, and he carried me to the river of honey, and I saw there Isaiah and Jeremiah and Ezekiel and Amos, and Micah and Zechariah, the minor and major prophets, and they saluted me in the city. I said to the angel: What way is this? And he said to me: This is the way of the prophets, every one who shall have afflicted his soul and not done his own will because of God, when he shall have gone out of the world and have been led to the Lord God and adored him, then by the command of God he is handed over to Michael, and he leads him into the city to this place of the prophets, and they salute him as their friend and neighbour because he did the will of God.

26. Again he led me where there is a river of milk, and I saw in that place all the infants whom Herod slew because of the name of Christ, and they saluted me, and the angel said to me: All who keep their chastity with purity, when they shall have come out of the body, after they adore the Lord God are delivered to Michael and are led to the infants and they salute them, saying that they are our brothers and friends and members; in themselves they shall inherit the promises of God.

27. Again he took me up and carried me to the north of the city and led me where there was a river of wine, and there I saw Abraham and Isaac and Jacob, Lot and Job and other saints, and they saluted me: and I asked and said: What is this place, my Lord? The angel answered and said to me: All who are receivers of pilgrims, when they go out of the world, first adore the Lord God, and are delivered to Michael and by this way are led into the city, and all the just salute him as son and brother, and say unto him: Because thou hast observed humanity and the receiving of pilgrims, come, have an inheritance in the city of the Lord our God: every just man shall receive good things of God in the city, according to his own action.

28. And again he carried me near the river of oil on the east of the city. And I saw there men rejoicing and singing psalms, and I said: Who are those, my Lord? And the angel saith to me: Those are they who devoted themselves to God with their whole heart and had no pride in themselves. For all those who rejoice in the Lord God and sing psalms to the Lord with their whole heart are here led into this city.

29. And he carried me into the midst of the city near the twelve walls. But there was in this place a higher wall, and I asked and said: Is there in the City of Christ a wall which in honour exceeds this place? And the angel answering said to me: There is a second better than the first, and similarly a third than the second, as each exceeds the other, unto the twelfth wall. And I said: Tell me, Sir, why one exceeds another in glory? And the angel answered and said unto me: All who have in themselves even a little detraction or zeal or pride, something of his glory would be made void even if he were in the city of Christ: look backward!

And turning round I saw golden thrones placed in each gate, and on them men having golden diadems and gems: and I looked carefully and I saw inside between the twelve men thrones placed in another rank which appeared of much glory, so that no one is able to recount their praise. And I asked the angel and said: My lord, who is on the throne? And the angel answered and said unto me: Those thrones belong to those who had goodness and understanding of heart and made themselves fools for the sake of the Lord God, nor knew new Scriptures nor psalms, but, mindful of one chapter of the commands of God, and hearing what it contained they wrought thereby in much diligence and had s fight zeal before the Lord God, and the admiration of them will seize all the saints in presence of the Lord God, for talking with one another they say, Wait and see the unlearned who know nothing more: by which means they merited so great and such a garment and so great glory on account of their innocence.

And I saw in the midst of this city a great altar, very high, and there was one standing near the altar whose countenance shone as the sun, and he held in his hands a psaltery and harp, and he sang psalms, saying Halleluia! And his voice filled the whole city: at the same time when all they who were on the towers and gates heard him they responded Halleluia! so that the foundations of the city were shaken: and I asked the angel and said, Sir, who is this of so great power? And the angel said to me: This is David: this is the city of Jerusalem, for when Christ the King of Eternity shall come with the assurance of His kingdom, he again shall go before him that he may sing psalms, and all the just at the same time shall sing psalms responding Halleluia! And I said, Sir, how did David alone above the other saints make a beginning of psalm-singing? And the angel answered and said unto me: Because Christ the Son of God sits at the right hand of His Father, and this David sings psalms before him in the seventh heaven, and as is done in the heavens so also below, because the host may not be offered to God without David, but it is necessary that David should sing psalms in the hour of the oblation of the body and blood of Christ: as it is performed in heaven so also on earth.

30. And I said to the angel: Sir, what is Alleluia? And the angel answered and said to me: You ask questions about everything. And he said to me, Alleluia is said in the Hebrew language of God and angels, for the meaning of Alleluia is this: *tecel cat. marith macha.* And I said, Sir, what is *tecel cat. marith macha?* And the angel answered and said unto me: *tecel'cat. marith macha* is: Let us all bless him together. I asked the angel and

said, Sir, do all who say Alleluia bless the Lord? And the angel answered and said to me: It is so, and again, therefore, if any one sing Alleluia and those who are present do not sing at the same time, they commit sin because they do not sing along with him, And I said: My lord, does he also sin if he be hesitating or very old? The angel answered and said unto me: Not so, but he who is able and does not join in the singing, know such as a despiser of the Word, and it would be proud and unworthy that he should not bless the Lord God his maker.

31. Moreover when he had ceased speaking to me, he led me outside the city through the midst of the trees and far from the places of the land of the good, and put me across the river of milk and honey: and after that he led me over the ocean which supports the foundations of heaven.

The angel answered and said unto me: Dost thou understand why thou goest hence? And I said: Yes, sir. And he said to me Come and follow me, and I will show thee the souls of the impious and sinners, that thou mayest know what manner of place it is. And I proceeded with the angel and he carried me by the setting of the sun, and I saw the beginning of heaven rounded on a great river of water, and I asked: What is this river of water? And he said to me: This is Ocean which surrounds all the Earth. And when I was at the outer limit of Ocean I looked, and there was no light in that place, but darkness and sorrow and sadness: and I sighed.

And I saw there a fervent river of fire, and in it a multitude of men and women immersed. up to the knees, and other men up to the navel, others even up to the lips, others moreover up to the hair. And I asked the angel and said: Sir, who are those in the fiery river? And the angel answered and said to me: They are neither hot nor cold, because they were found neither in the number of the just nor in the number of the impious. For those spent the time of their life on earth passing some days in prayer, but others in sins and fornications, until their death. And I asked him and said: Who are these, Sir, immersed up to their knees in fire? He answered and said to me: These are they who when they have gone out of church throw themselves into strange conversations to dispute. Those indeed who are immersed up to the navel are those who, when they have taken the body and blood of Christ go and fornicate and did not cease from their sins till they died. Those who are immersed up to the lips are the detractors of each other when they assemble in the church of God: those up to the eyebrows are those who nod approval of themselves and plot spite against their neighbour.

32. And I saw on the north a place of various and diverse punishments full of men and women, and a river of fire ran down into it. Moreover I observed and I saw pits great in depth, and in them several souls together, and the depth of that place was as it were three thousand cubits, and I saw them groaning and weeping and saying: Have pity on us, O Lord! and none had pity on them. And I asked the angel and said: Who are these, Sir? And the angel answered and said unto me: These are they who did not hope in the Lord, that they would be able to have him as their helper. And I asked and said: Sir, if these souls remain for thirty or forty generations thus one upon another, if

they were sent deeper, the pits I believe would not hold them. And he said to me: The Abyss has no measure, for beyond this it stretches down below him who is down in it: and so it is, that if perchance anyone should take a stone and throw it into a very deep well and after many hours it should reach the bottom, such is the abyss. For when the souls are thrown in there, they hardly reach the bottom in fifty years.

33. I, indeed, when I heard this, wept and groaned over the human race. The angel answered and said unto me: Why dost thou weep? Art thou more pitiful than God? For though God is good, He knows also that there are punishments, and He patiently bears with the human race, dismissing each one to work his own will in the time in which he dwells on the earth.

34. I further observed the fiery river and saw there a man being tortured by Tartaruchian angels having in their hands an iron with three hooks with which they pierced the bowels of that old man: and I asked the angel, and said: Sir, who is that old man on whom such torments are imposed? And the angel answered and said to me: He whom you see was a presbyter who did not perform well his ministry: when he had been eating and drinking and committing fornication he offered the host to the Lord at his holy altar.

35. And I saw not far away another old man led on by malign angels running with speed, and they pushed him into the fire up to his knees, and they struck him with stones and wounded his face like a storm, and did not allow him to say: Have pity on me! And I asked the angel and he said to me: He

whom you see was a bishop, and did not perform well his episcopate, who indeed accepted the great name but did not enter into the witness of him who gave him the name in all his life, seeing that he did not do just judgment, and did not pity widows and orphans, but now he receives retribution according to his iniquity and his works.

36. And I saw another man in the fiery river up to his knees. Moreover his hands were stretched out and bloody, and worms proceeded from his mouth and nostrils and he was groaning and weeping, and crying he said: Have pity on me! for I am hurt above the rest who are in this punishment. And I asked, Sir, who is this? And he said to me: This man whom thou seest, was a deacon who devoured the oblations and committed fornications and did not right in the sight of God, for this cause he unceasingly pays this penalty.

And I looked closely and saw alongside of him another man whom they delivered up with haste and cast into the fiery river, and he was (in it) up to the knees: and there came the angel who was set over the punishments having a great fiery razor, and with it he cut the lips of that man and the tongue likewise. And sighing, I lamented and asked: Who is that, sir. And he said to me, He whom thou seest was a reader and read to the people, but he himself did not keep the precepts of God: now he also pays the proper penalty.

37. And I saw another multitude of pits in the same place, and in the midst of it a river full of a multitude of men and women, and worms consumed them. But I lamented and

sighing asked the angel and said: Sir, who are these? And he said to me: These are those who exacted interest on interest and trusted in their riches and did not hope in God that He was their helper.

And after that I looked and saw another place, very narrow, and it was like a wall, and fire round about it. And I saw inside men and women gnawing their tongues, and I asked: Sir, who are these. And he said to me: These are they who in church disparage the Word of God, not attending to it, but as it were make naught of God and His angels: for that cause they now likewise pay the proper penalty.

38. And I observed and saw another old man down in a pit and his countenance was like blood, and I asked and said, Sir, what is this place? And he said to me: Into that pit stream all the punishments. And I saw men and women immersed up to the lips and I asked, Sir, who are these? And he said to me: These are the magicians who prepared for men and women evil magic arts and did not find how to stop them till they died.

And again I saw men and women with very black faces in a pit of fire, and I sighed and lamented and asked, Sir, who are these? And he said to me: These are fornicators and adulterers who committed adultery having wives of their own: likewise also the women committed adultery having husbands of their own: therefore they unceasingly suffer penalties.

39. And I saw there girls having black raiment, and four terrible angels having in their hands burning chains, and they

put them on the necks of the girls and led them into darkness: and I, again weeping, asked the angel: Who are these, Sir? And he said to me: These are they who, when they were virgins, defiled their virginity unknown to their parents; for which cause they unceasingly pay the proper penalties.

And again I observed there men and women with hands cut and their feet placed naked in a place of ice and snow, and worms devoured them. But seeing them I lamented and asked: Sir, who are these? And he said to me: These are they who harmed orphans and widows and the poor, and did not hope in the Lord, for which cause they unceasingly pay the proper penalties.

And I observed and saw others hanging over a channel of water, and their tongues were very dry, and many fruits were placed in their sight, and they were not permitted to take of them, and I asked: Sir, who are these? And he said to me: These are they who break their fast before the appointed hour, for this cause they unceasingly pay these penalties.

And I saw other men and women hanging by their eyebrows and their hair, and a fiery river drew them, and I said: Who are these, my Lord? And he said to me: These are they who join themselves not to their own husbands and wives but to whores, and therefore they unceasingly pay the proper penalties.

And I saw other men and women covered with dust, and their countenance was like blood, and they were in a pit of pitch and sulphur and running down into a fiery river, and I asked: Sir, who are these? And he said to me: These are they who committed the iniquity of Sodom and Gomorrah, the male with the male, for which reason they unceasingly pay the penalties.

40. And I observed and saw men and women clothed in bright garments, having their eyes blind, placed in a pit, and I asked: Sir, who are these? And he said to me: These are of the people who did alms, and knew not the Lord God, for which reason they unceasingly pay the proper penalties. And I observed and saw other men and women on an obelisk of fire, and beasts tearing them in pieces, and they were not allowed to say, Lord have pity on us! And I saw the angel of penalties putting heavy punishments on them and saying: Acknowledge the Son of God; for this was predicted to you, when the divine Scriptures were read to you, and you did not attend; for which cause God's judgment is just, for your actions have apprehended you and brought you into these penalties. But I sighed and wept, and I asked and said: Who are these men and women who are strangled in fire and pay their penalties? And he answered me: These are women who defiled the image of God when bringing forth infants out of the womb, and these are the men who lay with them. And their infants addressed the Lord God and the angels who were set over the punishments, saying: Cursed be the hour to our parents, for they defiled the image of God, having the name of God but not observing His precepts: they gave us for food to dogs and to be trodden down of swine: others they threw into the river. But their infants were handed over to the angels of Tartarus who were set over the punishments, that they might lead them to a wide place of

mercy: but their fathers and mothers were tortured in a perpetual punishment.

And after that I saw men and women clothed with rags full of pitch and fiery sulphur, and dragons were coiled about their necks and shoulders and feet, and angels having fiery horns restrained them and smote them, and closed their nostrils, saying to them: Why did ye not know the time in which it was right to repent and serve God, and did not do it? And I asked: Sir, who are these? And he said to me: These are they who seem to give up the world for God, putting on our garb, but the impediments of the world made them wretched, not maintaining *agapae* , and they did not pity widows and orphans: they did not receive the stranger and the pilgrim, nor did they offer the oblations, and they did not pity their neighbour. Moreover their prayer did not even on one day ascend pure to the Lord God, but many impediments of the world detained them, and they were not able to do right in the sight of God, and the angels enclosed them in the place of punishments. Moreover they saw those who were in punishments and said to them: We indeed when we lived in the world neglected God, and ye also did likewise: as we also truly when we were in the world knew that ye were sinners. But ye said: These are just and servants of God, now we know why ye were called by the name of the Lord: for which cause they also pay their own penalties.

And sighing I wept and said: Woe unto men, woe unto sinners! why were they born? And the angel answered and said unto me: Why dost thou lament? Art thou more pitiful than the Lord God who is blessed forever, who established judgment and sent forth every man to choose good and evil in his own will and do what pleases him? Then I lamented again very greatly, and he said to me: Dost thou lament when as yet thou hast not seen greater punishments? Follow me and thou shalt see seven times greater than these.

41. And he carried me south and placed me above a well, and I found it sealed with seven seals: and answering, the angel who was with me said to the angel of that place: Open the mouth of the well that Paul, the well-beloved of God, may see, for authority is given him that he may see all the pains of hell. And the angel said to me: Stand afar off that thou mayest be able to bear the stench of this place. When therefore the well was opened, immediately there arose from it a certain hard and malign stench, which surpasses all punishments: and I looked into the well and I saw fiery masses glowing in every. part, and narrow places, and the mouth of the well was narrow so as to admit one man only. And the angel answered and said unto me: If any man shall have been put into this well of the abyss and it shall have been sealed over him, no remembrance of him shall ever be made in the sight of the Father and His Son and the holy angels. And I said: Who are these, Sir, who are put into this well? And he said to me: They are whoever shall not confess that Christ has come in the flesh and that the Virgin Mary brought him forth, and whoever says that the bread and cup of the Eucharist of blessing are not this body and blood of Christ.

42. And I looked to the south in the west and I saw there a restless worm and in that place there was gnashing of teeth:

moreover the worms were one cubit long, and had two heads, and there I saw men and women in cold and gnashing of teeth. And I asked and said, Sir, who are these in this place? And he said to me: These are they who say that Christ did not rise from the dead and that this flesh will not rise again. And I asked and said: Sir, is there no fire nor heat in this place? And he said to me: In this place there is nothing else but cold and snow: and again he said to me: Even if the sun should rise upon them, they do not become warm on account of the superabundant cold of that place and the snow.

But hearing these things I stretched out my hands and wept, and sighing again, I said: It were better for us if we had not been born, all of us who are sinners.

43. But when those who were in the same place saw me weeping with the angel, they themselves cried out and wept saying, Lord God have mercy upon us! And after these things I saw the heavens open, and Michael the archangel descending from heaven, and with him was the whole army of angels, and they came to those who were placed in punishment and seeing him, again weeping, they cried out and said, Have pity on as! Michael the archangel, have pity on us and on the human race, for on account of thy prayers the earth standeth. We now see the judgment and acknowledge the Son of God! It was impossible for us before these things to pray for this, before we entered into this place: for we heard that there was a judgment before we went out of the world, but impediments and the life of the world did not allow us to repent. And Michael answered and said: Hear Michael speaking! I am he who stands in the

sight of God every. hour: As the Lord liveth, in whose sight I stand, I do not intermit one day or one night praying incessantly for the human race, and I indeed pray for those who are on the earth: but they do not cease doing iniquity and fornications, and they do not bring to me any good while they are placed on earth: and ye have consumed in vanity the time in which ye ought to have repented. But I have always prayed thus and I now beseech that God may send dew and send forth rains upon the earth, and now I desire until the earth produce its fruits and verily I say, that if any have done but a little good, I will agonise for him, protecting him till he have escaped the judgment of penalties. Where therefore are your prayers? Where are your penances? Ye have lost your time contemptuously. But now weep and I will weep with you and the angels who are with me with the well-beloved Paul, if perchance the merciful God will have pity and give you refreshment. But hearing these words they cried out and wept greatly, and all said with one voice: Have pity on us, Son of God! And I, Paul, sighed and said: O Lord God! have pity on thy creature, have pity on the sons of men, have pity on thine image.

44. And I looked and saw the heaven move like a tree shaken by the wind. Suddenly, moreover, they threw, themselves on their faces in the sight of the throne. And I saw twenty-four elders and twenty-four thousand adoring God, and I saw an altar and veil and throne, and all were rejoicing; and the smoke of a good odour was raised near the altar of the throne of God, and I heard the voice of one saying: For the sake of what do ye our angels and ministers intercede? And they cried out saying: We intercede seeing thy many kindnesses to

the human race. And after these things I saw the Son of God descending from heaven, and a diadem was on his head. And seeing him those who were placed in punishment exclaimed all with one voice saying: Have pity, Son of the High God! Thou art He who shewest refreshment for all in the heavens and on earth, and on us likewise have pity, for since we have seen Thee, we have refreshment. And a voice went out from the Son of God through all the punishments saying: And what work have ye done that ye demand refreshment from me? My blood was poured out for your sakes, and not even so did ye repent: for your sakes I wore the crown of thorns on my head: for you I received buffets on my cheeks, and not even so did ye repent. I asked water when hanging on the cross and they gave me vinegar mixed with gall, with a spear they opened my right side, for my name's sake they slew my prophets and just men, and in all these things I gave you a place of repentance and ye would not. Now, however, for the sake of Michael the archangel of my covenant and the angels who are with him, and because of Paul the well-beloved, whom I would not vex, for the sake of your brethren who are in the world and offer oblations, and for the sake of your sons, because my precepts are in them, and more for the sake of mine own kindness, on the day on which I rose from the dead, I give to you all who are in punishment a night and a day of refreshment forever. And they all cried out and said, We bless thee, Son of God, that Thou hast given us a night and a day of respite. For better to us is a refreshment of one day above all the time of our life which we were on earth, and if we had plainly known that this was intended for those who sin, we would have worked no other work, we would have done no business, and we would have done no iniquity: what need had we for pride in the world? For here our pride is crushed which ascended from our mouth against our neighbour: our plagues and excessive straitness and the tears and the worms which are under us, these are much worse to us than the pains which we have left behind us. When they said thus, the malign angels of the penalties were angered with them, saying: How long do ye lament and sigh? for ye had no pity. For this is the judgment of God who had no pity. But ye received this great grace of a day and a night's refreshment on the Lord's Day for the sake of Paul the well-beloved of God who descended to you.

45. And after that the angel said to me: Hast thou seen all these things? And I said: Yes, Sir. And he said to me: Follow me and I will lead thee into Paradise, that the just who are there may see thee, for lo! they hope to see thee, and they are ready to come to meet thee in joy and gladness. And I followed the angel by the impulse of the Holy Spirit, and he placed me in Paradise and said to me: This is Paradise in which Adam and his wife erred. Moreover I entered Paradise and saw the beginning of waters, and there was an angel making a sign to me and he said to me: Observe, said he, the waters, for this is the river of Physon which surrounds all the land of Evilla, and the second is Geon which surrounds all the land of Egypt and Ethiopia, and the third is Thigris which is over against the Assyrians, and another is Eufrates which waters all the land of Mesopotamia. And when I had gone inside I saw a tree planted from whose roots water flowed out, and from this beginning there were four rivers. And the spirit of God rested on that tree, and when the Spirit blew, the waters flowed forth, and I said:

My Lord, is it this tree itself which makes the waters flow? And he said to me: That from the beginning, before the heavens and earth were manifested, and all things here invisible, the Spirit of God was borne upon the waters, but from the time when the command of God made the heavens and earth to appear, the Spirit rested upon this tree: wherefore whenever the Spirit blows, the waters flow forth from the tree. And he held me by the hand and led me near the tree of knowledge of good and evil, and he said: This is the tree by which death entered into the world, and receiving of it through his wife Adam ate and death entered into the world. And he shewed me another tree in the midst of Paradise, and saith to me: This is the tree of life.

46. While I was yet looking upon the tree, I saw a virgin coming from afar and two hundred angels before her saying hymns, and I asked and said: Sir, who is she who comes in so great glory? And he said to me: This is Mary the Virgin, the Mother of the Lord. And coming near she saluted me and said: Hail, Paul! well-beloved of God and angels and men. For all the saints prayed my Son Jesus who is my Lord that thou mightest come hither in the body that they might see thee before thou goest out of the world. And the Lord said to them: Bear and be patient: yet a little and ye shall see him and he shall be with you for ever: and again they all said to him together: Do not vex us, for we desire to see him in the flesh, for by him Thy name was greatly glorified in the world, and we have seen that he endured all the labours whether of the greater or of the less. This we learn from those who come hither. For when we say: Who is he who directed you in the world? they reply to us: There is one in the world whose name is Paul, he preaches and announces

Christ, and we believe that many have entered into the kingdom through the virtue and sweetness of his speeches. Behold all the just men are behind me coming to meet thee, Paul, and I first come for this cause to meet them who did the will of my Son and my Lord Jesus Christ, I first advance to meet them and do not send them away to be as wanderers until they meet in peace.

47. When she had thus spoken, I saw three coming from afar, very beautiful in the likeness of Christ, and their forms were shining, and their angels, and I asked: Sir, who are these? And he said to me: Dost thou not know those? And I said: No, Sir. And he answered: These are the fathers of the people, Abraham, Isaac, and Jacob. And coming near they saluted me, and said: Hail, Paul, well-beloved of God and men; blessed is he who suffers violence for the Lord's sake. And Abraham answered me and said: This is my son Isaac, and Jacob my well-beloved, and we have known the Lord and followed him; blessed are all they who believed in thy word, that they may be able to inherit the Kingdom of God by labour, by renunciation, and sanctification, and humility, and charity, and meekness, and fight faith in the Lord; and we also have had devotion to the Lord whom thou preachest in the testament, that we might assist those who believed in him with their whole soul, and might minister unto them as fathers minister to their children.

When they had thus spoken, I saw other twelve coming from afar in honour, and I asked: Sir, who are these? And he said: These are the patriarchs. And coming near they saluted me and said: Hail, Paul, well-beloved of God and men: the Lord did not vex us, that we might see thee yet in the body, before thou goest out of the world. And each one of them reminded me of his name in order, from Ruben to Benjamin: and Joseph said to me: I am he who was sold; but I say to thee, Paul, that all the things, whatever my brothers did to me, in nothing did I act maliciously with them, nor in all the labour which they imposed on me, nor in any point was I hurt by them on that account from morning till evening: blessed is he who receives some hurt on account of the Lord, and bears it, for the Lord will repay it to him manifold, when he shall have gone out of the world.

48. When he had spoken thus far, I saw another beautiful one coming from afar, and his angels saying hymns, and I asked: Sir, who is this that is beautiful of countenance? And he saith to me: Dost thou not know him? And I said: No, Sir. And he said to me: This is Moses the law-giver, to whom God gave the law. And when he had come near me, he immediately wept, and after that he saluted me: and I said to him: What dost thou lament? for I have heard that thou excellest every. man in meekness. And he answered saying: I weep for those whom I planted with toil, because they did not bear fruit, nor did any profit by them; and I saw all the sheep whom I fed, that they were scattered and become as if they had no shepherd, and because all the toils which I endured for the sake of the sons of Israel were accounted as naught, and how greatso-ever virtues I did in the midst of them these they did not understand, and I wonder that strangers and uncircumcised and idol-worshippers have been converted and have entered into the promises of God, but Israel has not entered; and now I say unto thee,

brother Paul, that in that hour when the people hanged Jesus whom thou preachest, that the Father, the God of all, who gave me the law, and Michael and all the angels and archangels, and Abraham and Isaac, and Jacob, and all the just wept over the Son of God hanging on the cross. In that hour all the saints attended on me looking (upon me) and they said to me: See, Moses, what men of thy people have done to the Son of God. Wherefore thou art blessed, Paul, and blessed the generation and race which believed in thy word.

49. When he had spoken thus far, there came other twelve, and seeing me said: Art thou Paul the glorified in heaven and on earth? And I answered and said: What are ye? The first answered and said: I am Esaias whom Manasses cut asunder with a wooden saw. And the second said likewise: I am Jeremias who was stoned by the children of Israel and slain. And the third said: I am Ezekiel whom the children of Israel dragged by the feet over a rock in a mountain till they knocked out my brains, and we endured all these toils, wishing to save the children of Israel: and I say unto thee that after the toils which they laid upon me, I cast myself on my face in the sight of the Lord praying for them, bending my knees until the second hour of the Lord's day, till Michael came and lifted me up from the earth. Blessed art thou, Paul, and blessed the nation which believed through thee.

And as these passed by, I saw another, beautiful of countenance, and I asked: Sir, Who is this? Who when he had seen me, rejoiced and said to me: This is Lot who was found just in Sodom. And approaching he saluted me and said:

Blessed art thou, Paul, and blessed the generation to which thou didst minister. And I answered and said to him: Art thou Lot who wast found just in Sodom? And he said: I entertained angels, as travellers, and when they of the city wished to violate them, I offered them my two virgin daughters who had not yet known men, and gave them to them saying: use them as ye will, but only to these men ye shall do no evil; for this cause they entered under the roof of my house. For this cause, therefore, we ought to be confident and know that if anyone shall have done anything, God shall repay him manifold when they shall come to him. Blessed art thou, Paul, and blessed the nation which believed in thy word.

When, therefore, he had ceased talking to me, I saw another coming from a distance, very beautiful of countenance, and smiling, and his angels saying hymns: and I said to the angel who was with me: Has then each of the just an angel for companion? And he said to me: Each one of the saints has his own (angel) assisting him, and saying a hymn, and the one does not depart from the other. And I said: Who is this, Sir? And he said: This is Job. And approaching, he saluted me and said: Brother Paul, thou hast great praise with God and men. And I am Job, who laboured much for a period of thirty years from a plague in the blood; and verily in the beginning, the wounds which went forth from my body were like grains of wheat. But on the third day, they became as the foot of an ass; worms moreover which fell four digits in length: and on the third (day) the devil appeared and said to me: Say something against God and die. I said to him: If such be the will of God that I should remain under a plague all the time of my life till I die, I shall not cease from blessing the Lord, and I shall receive more reward. For I know that the labours of that world are nothing to the refreshment which is afterwards: for which cause blessed art thou, Paul, and blessed the nation which believed through thee.

50. When he had spoken thus far, another came calling from afar and saying: Blessed art thou, Paul, and blessed am I because I saw thee, the beloved of the Lord. And I asked the angel: Sir, who is this? And he answered and said unto me: This is Noe in the time of the deluge. And immediately we saluted each other: and greatly rejoicing he said to me: Thou art Paul the most beloved of God. And I asked him: Who art thou? And he said: I am Noe, who was in the time of the deluge. And I say to thee, Paul, that working for a hundred years, I made the ark, not putting off the tunic with which I was clad, nor did I cut the hair of my head. Till then also I cherished continence, not approaching my own wife: in those hundred years not a hair of my head grew in length, nor did my garments become soiled: and I besought men at all times saying: Repent, for a deluge of waters will come upon you. But they laughed at me, and mocked my words; and again they said to me: But this is the time of those who are able to play and sin freely, desiring her with whom it is possible to commit fornication frequently: for God does not regard this, and does not know what things are done by us men, and there is no flood of waters straightway coming upon this world. And they did not cease from their sins, till God destroyed all flesh which had the breath of life in it. Know then that God loveth one just man more than all the world of the impious. Wherefore, blessed art thou, Paul, and blessed is the nation which believes through thee.

51. And turning round, I saw other just ones coming from afar, and I asked the angel: Sir, who are those? And he answered me: These are Elias and Eliseus. And they saluted me: and I said to them: Who are ye? And one of them answered and said: I am Elias, the prophet of God; I am Elias who prayed, and because of my word, the heaven did not rain for three years and six months, on account of the unrighteousness of men. God is just and true, who doeth the will of his servants: for the angels often besought the Lord for rain, and he said: Be patient till my servant Elias shall pray and petition for this and I will send rain on the earth.

The End of the Vision of Saint Paul

www.ingramcontent.com/pod-product-compliance
Lightning Source LLC
LaVergne TN
LVHW041501070426
835507LV00009B/740